The Joy of Dancing Through the Ages

T0087871

From Minuet To Rock

Selected and edited by Denes Agay

Yorktown Music Press, Inc.
New York/London/Paris/Sydney/Copenhagen/Berlin/Tokyo/Madrid

Cover illustration by Janice Fried
Project Editor: Felipe Orozco

This book Copyright © 2005 by Yorktown Music Press, Inc.

All rights reserved. No part of this book may be
reproduced in any form or by any electronic or mechanical means,
including information storage and retrieval systems,
without permission in writing from the publisher.

Order No. YK 21967
International Standard Book Number: 0.8256.8112.X

Exclusive Distributors:
Music Sales Corporation
257 Park Avenue South, New York, NY 10010 USA
Music Sales Limited
8/9 Frith Street, London W1D 3JB England
Music Sales Pty. Limited
120 Rothschild Street, Rosebery, Sydney, NSW 2018, Australia

Printed in the United States of America by
Vicks Lithograph and Printing Corporation

Table of Contents

Minuet . . . . . Ludwig van Beethoven (1770–1827) 4
Minuet . . . . . Luigi Boccherini (1743–1805) 6
Gavotte . . . . . Johann Sebastian Bach (1685-1750) 7
Three Ecossaises . . . . . Ludwig van Beethoven (1770–1827) 8
Two Ländler . . . . . Franz Schubert (1797–1828) 10
Polonaise . . . . . Michael K. Oginski (1765–1833) 12
Mazurka . . . . . Frédéric Chopin (1810–1849) 14
Polonaise Militaire . . . . . Frédéric Chopin (1810–1849) 16
Tarantella (La Danza) . . . . . Gioacchino Rossini (1792–1868) 19
Csárdás (Hungarian Folk Dance) . . . . . Traditional 22
The "Flédermaus" Polka . . . . . Johann Strauss II (1825–1899) 24
Waltzes by Strauss . . . . . Johann Strauss II (1825–1899) 26
Slavonic Dance No.8 . . . . . Antonín Dvořák (1841–1904) 28
Can-Can . . . . . Jacques Offenbach (1819–1880) 30
Valse Lente (Coppelia) . . . . . Léo Delibes (1836–1891) 32
Spanish Dance . . . . . Enrique Granados (1867–1916) 33
Cake-Walk . . . . . Kerry Mills (1869–1948) 36
The Entertainer . . . . . Scott Joplin (1868–1917) 38
Rumba Revels (La Cucaracha) . . . . . Denes Agay 41
Tango "La Cumparsita" . . . . . C.H. Matos Rodriguez 44
Alexander's Ragtime Band . . . . . Irving Berlin (1888–1989) 46
Nola . . . . . Felix Arndt 48
Boogie-Woogie ("Short'nin' Bread") . . . Denes Agay 50
Waltz from "Der Rosenkavalier" . . . . . Richard Strauss (1864–1949) 52
J.D.'s Boogie-Woogie . . . . . Jimmy Dorsey and Marvin Wright 54
Square Dance . . . . . Traditional 57
Clarinet Polka . . . . . Rev. by Denes Agay 60
Charleston . . . . . Cecil Mack and Jimmy Johnson 62
Palm Garden (Slow Blues) . . . . . Thomas "Fats" Waller (1904–1943) 64
Mardi Gras Bolero . . . . . Denes Agay 66
Hava Nagila . . . . . Traditional Israeli Folk Dance 69
Tuxedo Junction (Swing) . . . . . Hawkins – Johnson – Dash 70
Dizzy's Dilemma . . . . . Charlie Shavers (1917–1971) 72
Blowin' Hot and Cool . . . . . Gerald Martin 74
Another Shade of Blue . . . . . Denes Agay 76
The Happy Organ (Rock) . . . . . Wood – Clowney – Kriegsmann 78
Smoky on the Rocks . . . . . Gerald Martin 80

Minuet

Ludwig van Beethoven
(1770–1827)

Copyright © 2005 Yorktown Music Press, Inc.
All Rights Reserved. International Copyright Secured.

TRIO
p
mp
cresc.
f
dim.
1.
2.
D.C. senza ripetizione

Minuet

Copyright © 2005 Yorktown Music Press, Inc.
All Rights Reserved. International Copyright Secured.

Gavotte

Copyright © 2005 Yorktown Music Press, Inc.
All Rights Reserved. International Copyright Secured.

Three Ecossaises

Ludwig van Beethoven
(1770–1827)

Copyright © 2005 Yorktown Music Press, Inc.
All Rights Reserved. International Copyright Secured.

f
f
ff
3.
(Tranquillo)
p
f
f
ff

Two Ländler

Franz Schubert
(1797–1828)

Copyright © 2005 Yorktown Music Press, Inc.
All Rights Reserved. International Copyright Secured.

2.

Polonaise

Michael K. Oginski
(1765–1833)

Copyright © 2005 Yorktown Music Press, Inc.
All Rights Reserved. International Copyright Secured.

Trio
f staccato sempre
f
p espr.
mf
Ped. simile

Mazurka

Frédéric Chopin
(1810–1849)

Copyright © 2005 Yorktown Music Press, Inc.
All Rights Reserved. International Copyright Secured.

f
poco rit.
ten.
sf
pp
- a tempo
1-5
ten.
sf
pp
ten.
sf
pp
ten.
sf
rit.
a tempo
p
f
ff
poco rit.

Polonaise Militaire

Frédéric Chopin
(1810–1849)

Copyright © 2005 Yorktown Music Press, Inc.
All Rights Reserved. International Copyright Secured.

f
f
Ped. simile
con Ped.

mf
f
ff
mp
crescendo
f
p
ff
da Capo al fine
without repeats
Fine

Tarantella
(La Danza)

Gioacchino Rossini
(1792–1868)

Copyright © 2005 Yorktown Music Press, Inc.
All Rights Reserved. International Copyright Secured.

1.
2.
f
f
pp
f
p
f
p
f
sf
f
sf

sf
sf
sempre f
sf
f
f
f
sf
sf

Csárdás
(Hungarian Folk Dance)

Copyright © 2005 Yorktown Music Press, Inc.
All Rights Reserved. International Copyright Secured.

Dm
A7
Dm
C7
(2nd time faster)
C7
F
A7
Dm
A
Dm
Gm
Dm
A7
Dm
1.
2.
Gm
A7
Dm
f
f

The "Fledermaus" Polka

Johann Strauss II
(1825–1899)

Copyright © 2005 Yorktown Music Press, Inc.
All Rights Reserved. International Copyright Secured.

mp
a tempo
cresc.
f
f
Fine
mf
1.
2.
D.C. al Fine

Waltzes by Strauss

"The Emperor Waltz"

Johann Strauss II
(1825–1899)

Moderately

Copyright © 2005 Yorktown Music Press, Inc.
All Rights Reserved. International Copyright Secured.

"Wine, Women, and Song"

Slavonic Dance No. 8

Antonín Dvořák
(1841–1904)

Copyright © 2005 Yorktown Music Press, Inc.
All Rights Reserved. International Copyright Secured.

ff
p
ff
p
ff
p
pp
rit.
dim.
Presto
ff

Can-Can

From the Operetta "La Vie Parisienne"

Copyright © 2005 Yorktown Music Press, Inc.
All Rights Reserved. International Copyright Secured.

D.C. al Fine

Valse Lente
From Coppelia

Léo Delibes
(1836–1891)

Copyright © 2005 Yorktown Music Press, Inc.
All Rights Reserved. International Copyright Secured.

Spanish Dance
Playera-Andaluza (Danza Española Nº5)

Enrique Granados
(1867–1916)

Copyright © 1989 Unión Musical Ediciones, S.L. Madrid Spain
This arrangement © 2005 Unión Musical Ediciones, S.L. Madrid Spain
International Copyright Secured. All rights reserved

f

ff
f
mp

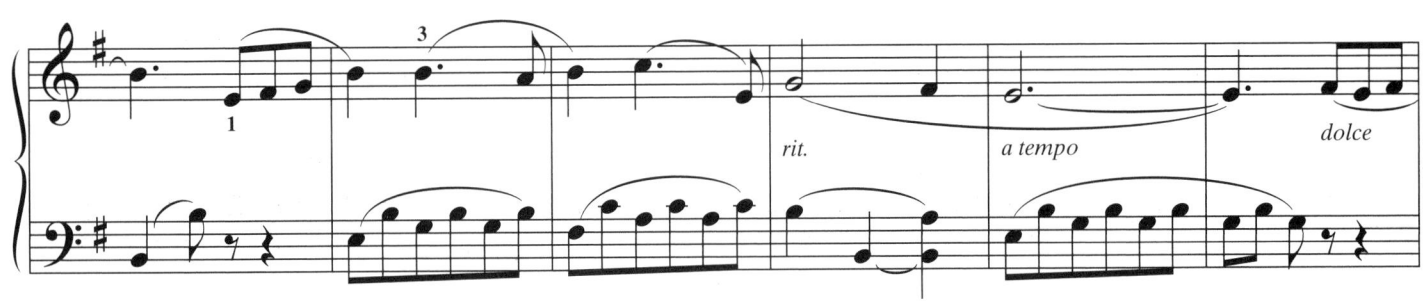
1
3
rit.
a tempo
dolce

to Coda
rall.
a tempo

Andante
5
f
mf
p
dim.
Tempo I
molto rit.
D.C. al Coda
Coda
rit.

Cake-Walk

Kerry Mills
(1869–1948)

Copyright © 2005 Yorktown Music Press, Inc.
All Rights Reserved. International Copyright Secured.

ff
sf

The Entertainer
Ragtime Two Step

Copyright © 2005 Yorktown Music Press, Inc.
All Rights Reserved. International Copyright Secured.

C
F
Fm
C
f
Cm
G
D7
G7
f
C
F
Fm
C
C7
mp
F
F♯dim
C
D7
G7
C
cresc.
f
C
C7
F
C
Dm
C
G7
C
f
C
C7
F
C
Cm
D7
G7
p
f

C
C7
F
C
Dm
C
G7
C
p
f
C7
F
Fm
C
G7
C
Dm
C
mf
G7
D♯dim
C
Dm
C
mf
F
Dm7
C
D♯dim
C
D7
G7
1.
C
2.
C
D.C. al Fine
cresc.
sf

Rumba Revels
(La Cucaracha)

Copyright © 2005 Yorktown Music Press, Inc.
All Rights Reserved. International Copyright Secured.

p
più f

ff
molto marcato il tema
p subito
f
p
ff

Tango "La Cumparsita"

Copyright © 2005 Yorktown Music Press, Inc.
All Rights Reserved. International Copyright Secured.

3
f
p
3
f
p
4
2
f

Alexander's Ragtime Band

Copyright © 2005 Yorktown Music Press, Inc.
All Rights Reserved. International Copyright Secured.

C
C7
F
am,
Hon - ey Lamb.
Come on a - long,
Come on a -
C7
F
B♭
long,
Let me take you by the hand,
Up to the man,
Up to the
man
who's the lead - er of the band,
And if you care to hear the
F C7 F
f
Cm7 F7 F75♯ B♭ G♯dim
Swa - nee Riv - er played in Rag - time,
Come on and
F G7 C9 C7 F
hear,
Come on and hear
Al - ex - an - der's Rag time Band.

Nola

Felix Arndt

Copyright © 2005 Yorktown Music Press, Inc.
All Rights Reserved. International Copyright Secured.

D7
G
D7
D75♯
G
D7
p
G
D
Fdim
A7
D7
(tacet)
G
D7
D75♯
G
D7
G7
C
Cm
G
C♯dim
G
C♯dim
D7
G
D.C.

Boogie-Woogie
("Short'nin' Bread")

Denes Agay

Copyright © 2005 Yorktown Music Press, Inc.
All Rights Reserved. International Copyright Secured.

p cantabile
f
sf
p non legato
crescendo
sempre
mf
cresc.
f
ff
decresc.
p
f
ff

Waltz from "Der Rosenkavalier"

Richard Strauss
(1864–1949)

Copyright © 2005 Yorktown Music Press, Inc.
All Rights Reserved. International Copyright Secured.

p
mf
cresc.
sempre
f
poco rit.
a tempo
p
accel.
dim.
f

J.D.'s Boogie-Woogie

Copyright © 1947 (Renewed) by Onyx Music Corporation
This arrangement © 2005 by Onyx Music Corporation
All Rights for Onyx Music Corporation administered by Music Sales Corporation (ASCAP)
International Copyright Secured. All rights reserved

F9
G7
C
f
F9
C
G7
F7
C
C7
mp
F7
poco
a poco cresc.

C7
G7
F7
C7
G7
f
F9
C
Dm7
F7
Cm6
C
G7
C
D♭9
C6
ff

Square Dance

Traditional

Copyright © 2005 Yorktown Music Press, Inc.
All Rights Reserved. International Copyright Secured.

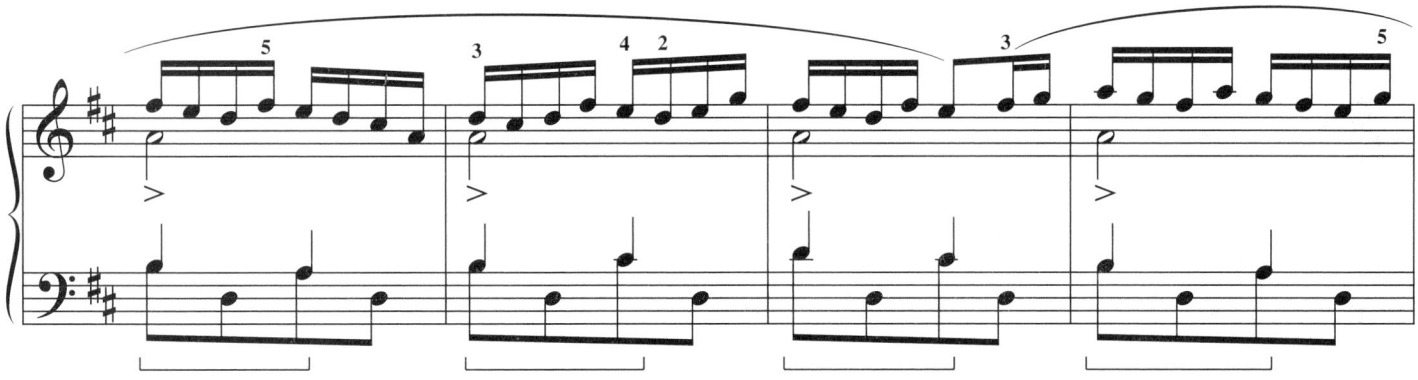

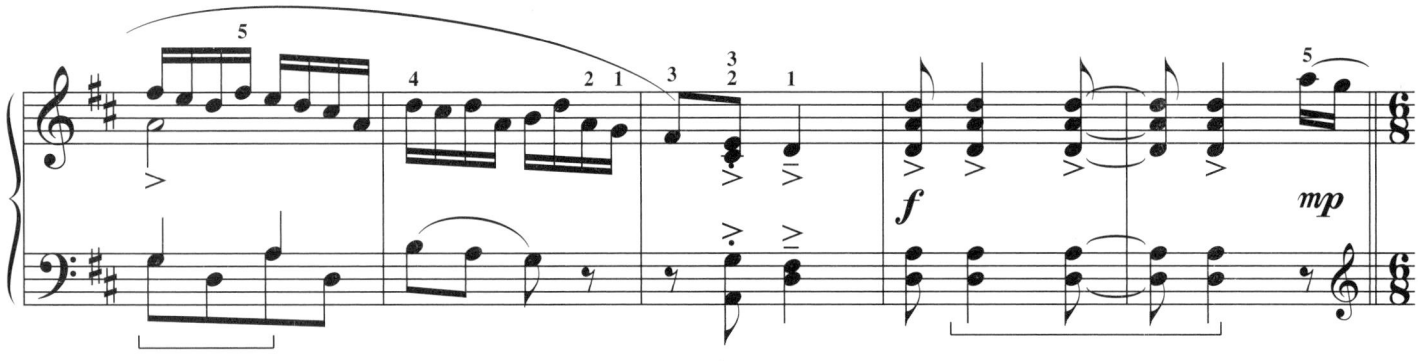

Irish Washerwoman
Allegro

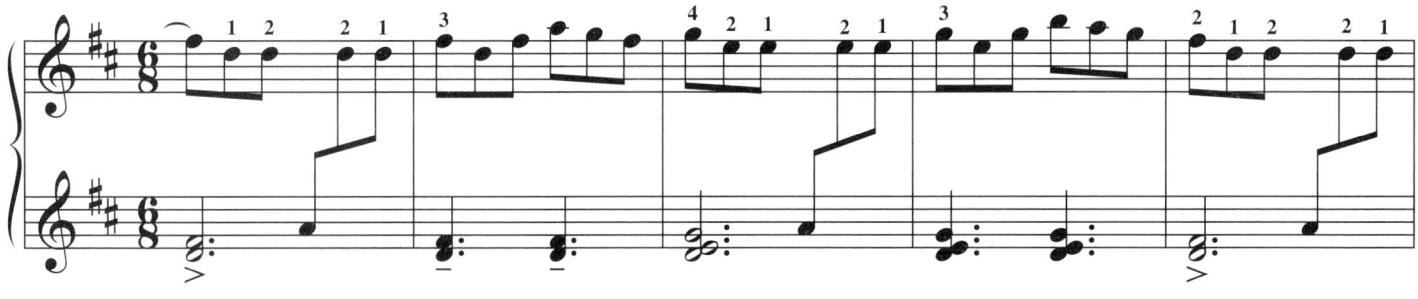

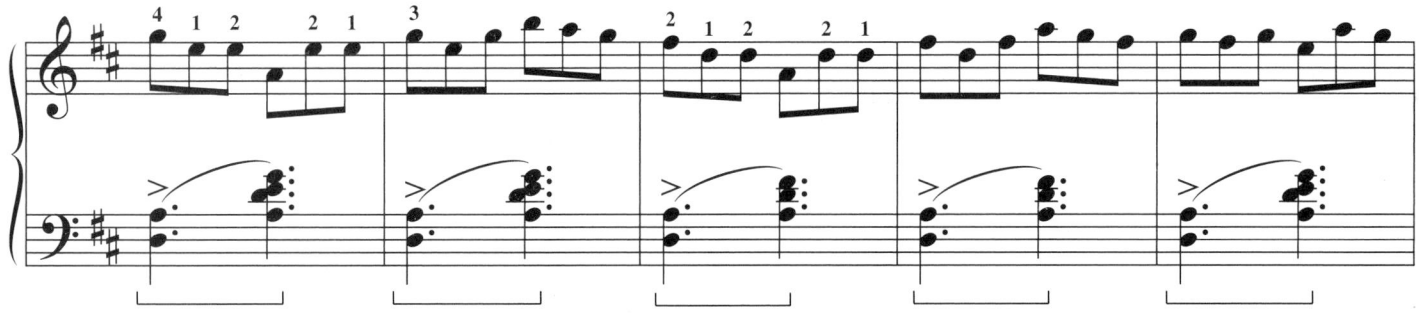

8
p
8
f
p
cresc.
ff

Clarinet Polka

Rev. by Denes Agay
(1911–)

Copyright © 2005 Yorktown Music Press, Inc.
All Rights Reserved. International Copyright Secured.

D.C.
Trio
f
f

Charleston

Cecil Mack and
Jimmy Johnson

© 1923 WARNER BROS. INC. (Renewed)
This Arrangement © 2005 WARNER BROS. INC.
All Rights Reserved. Used by Permission.

F7
B♭
D7
G7
C7
F9
B♭6
B♭dim
F7
Gm
B♭7
E♭
B♭
C75♭
B♭6
B♭dim
F7
B♭
E♭6
1.
B♭
B♭dim
F7
2.
B♭
fz

Palm Garden
(Slow Blues)

Thomas "Fats" Waller
(1904–1943)

© ANNE-RACHEL MUSIC CORPORATION (Renewed)
This Arrangement © 2005 ANNE-RACHEL MUSIC CORPORATION
All Rights Reserved. Used by Permission.

A♭7 G7 Cm7 F9 B♭7 E♭ B♭7 E♭ B7 Fm7 B♭9
E♭ D♭ E♭ Bm7 B♭m7 E♭7 A♭ D♭9
dim.
f
A♭ E♭7 A♭ Bdim B♭m7 E♭7 B♭m7 E♭7
B♭ D♭dim A♭ E♭9 A♭ tacet B♭ D♭dim A♭ B♭m A♭ tacet
mf
mp
B♭ D♭dim A♭ B♭m A♭ B♭m7 A♭ E♭7 A♭ E♭+5 A♭6
mf

Mardi Gras Bolero

Denes Agay

Copyright © 2005 Yorktown Music Press, Inc.
All Rights Reserved. International Copyright Secured.

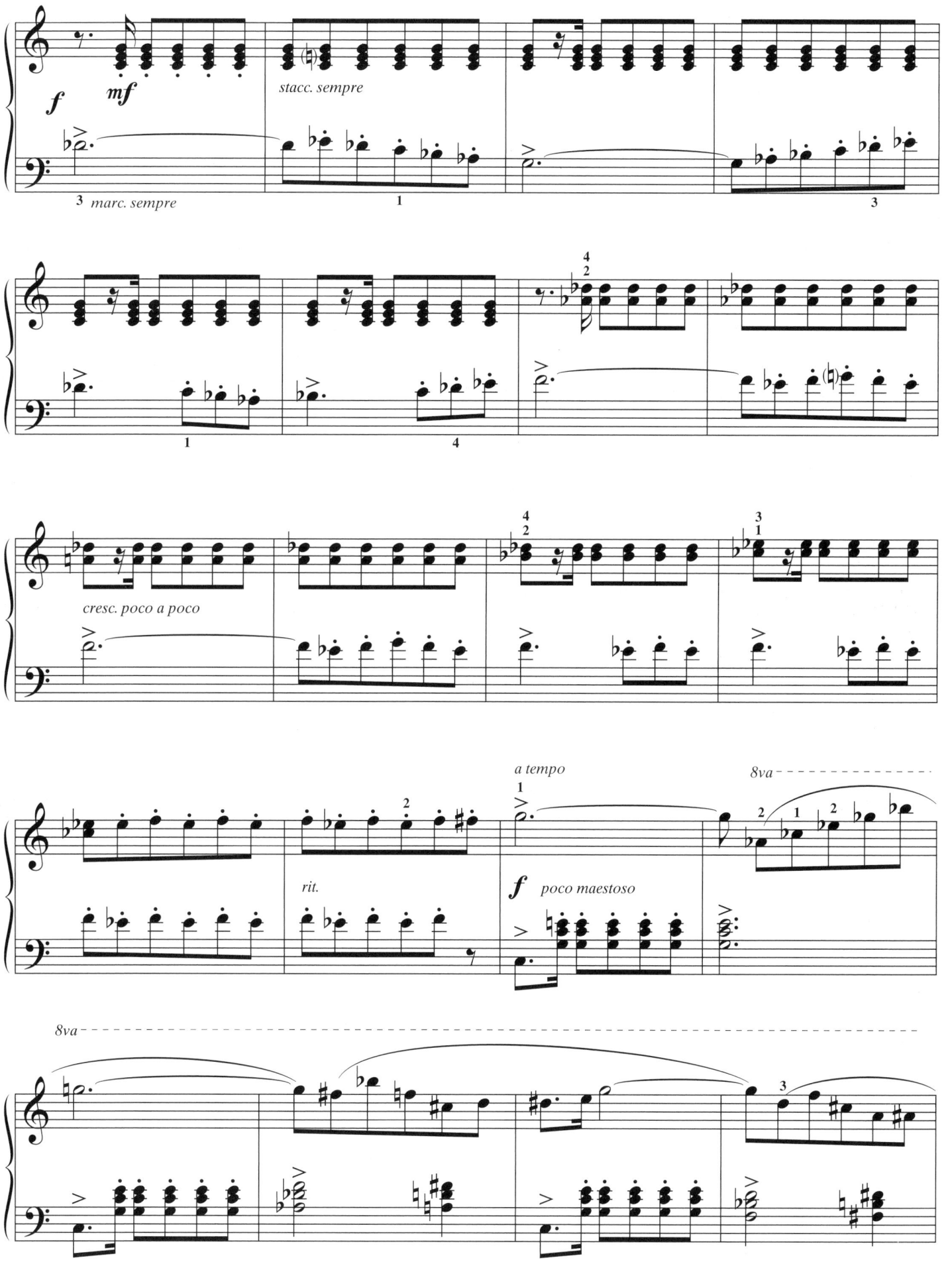
f
mf
stacc. sempre
marc. sempre
cresc. poco a poco
a tempo
8va
rit.
f
poco maestoso
8va

8va
p
dim.
p
cresc.
f
ff

Hava Nagila

Traditional Israeli Folk Dance

Copyright © 2005 Yorktown Music Press, Inc.
All Rights Reserved. International Copyright Secured.

Tuxedo Junction
(Swing)

Buddy Feyne, Erskine Hawkins,
William Johnson and Julian Dash

Copyright © 1940 (Renewed) Music Sales Corporation (ASCAP) and Rytvoc, Inc.
This arrangement © 2005 Music Sales Corporation (ASCAP) and Rytvoc, Inc.
International Copyright Secured. All Rights Reserved.

B♭
B♭7
E♭6
B♭6
f
E♭7
B♭7
E♭6
B♭6
Cm7
F7
B♭
E♭7
F7
B♭
E♭7
F7
B♭
E♭7
Edim
B♭
F7
1.
2.
B♭
B♭7
B♭
tacet
F75♭
B♭6

Dizzy's Dilemma

Copyright © 1946 (Renewed) by Music Sales Corporation (ASCAP)
This © arrangement 2005 by Music Sales Corporation (ASCAP)
International Copyright Secured. All Rights Reserved

Em B7 Em F7 Em B7 Em C
Em Am B7 Em Em6 F♯7
f
C7 F E
Dm6 Cm6 Bm6 Am6 C7 B7 Em B7 Em
mf
Em B7 Em F7 Em B7 Em C
Em Am B7 Em rit. C9 Em6

Blowin' Hot and Cool

Copyright © 2005 Yorktown Music Press, Inc.
All Rights Reserved. International Copyright Secured.

to Coda
A♭9 E9 G9♭ Cm6 C B♭ A♭ G7
f
mf
C B♭ A♭ G C B♭ A♭ G
C B♭ A♭ G C B♭ A♭ G7 C B♭
p
D.C. al Coda
A♭ G7 C B♭ Am G Dm7 G7 Dm7 G7
mf
p
Coda
C7(5♯) F9 D♭9 Cm9
f

Another Shade of Blue

Copyright © 2005 Yorktown Music Press, Inc.
All Rights Reserved. International Copyright Secured.

Poco più mosso
Em
Am6
C9
R.H.
mf molto cantabile
L.H.
B7♭5
D7
G7
Am
Em
Am
Fmaj7
E♭
rit.
f
Rather broadly
B7
Em
Em(maj7)
Em7
F♯7♭5
ff
(Tempo I)
Em
Am6
Em
Am6
Em
A
p
A♭
B7
Em
C7
Em
8va
dim.
rit.
pp

The Happy Organ
(Rock)

Ken Wood, David Clowney
and James J. Kriegsmann

Copyright © 1959 (Renewed) by Embassy Music Corporation (BMI)
This © arrangement 2005 by Embassy Music Corporation (BMI)
International Copyright Secured. All Rights Reserved

C
to Coda
C
mf
G7
C
F
G7
C
f
G7
F
C
D.S. 𝄋
Coda
C
mf
mp
p
pp

Smoky on the Rocks

Copyright © 2005 Yorktown Music Press, Inc.
All Rights Reserved. International Copyright Secured.